ITIL® Foundation Essentials
The exam facts you need

D0814387

ITIL® Foundation Essentials

The exam facts you need

CLAIRE AGUTTER

IT Governance Publishing

IT Governance Publishing
IT Governance Limited
Unit 3, Clive Court
Bartholomew's Walk
Cambridgeshire Business Park
Ely
Cambridgeshire
CB7 4EA
United Kingdom

www.itgovernance.co.uk

© Claire Agutter 2012
The author has asserted the rights of the author under the Copyright, Designs and Patents Act, 1988, to be identified as the author of this work.

First published in the United Kingdom in 2012 by IT Governance Publishing.

ISBN 978-1-84928-399-1

FOREWORD

Sometimes, when you're trying to learn a new subject, there is just so much information available to you that finding the starting point can be too daunting a task in itself.

The ITIL$^{®}$[1] service lifecycle is no exception, information is all around us: e-books, traditional paper books, the internet, blogs and opinions provided by friends and colleagues.

Where do you start?

Success in the ITIL Foundation certificate relies on the student understanding the concepts, principles and, most importantly, the language of the framework to enable an informed conversation with peers to take place.

This guide provides you, the student, with the information you need in a straightforward, easy to digest form, accompanied by explanatory diagrams and tables.

It doesn't take the place of accredited learning, either online or instructor led in the classroom, but it does give you an invaluable tool and the facts you need for success.

Rosemary Gurney
ITIL Trainer & Consultant at Global Knowledge Networks Ltd
Senior Examiner, with responsibility for Foundation Certificate – APM Group.

---

[1] ITIL$^{®}$ is a registered trademark of the Cabinet Office.

PREFACE

This book provides a handy revision guide for the ITIL Foundation Certificate in IT Service Management.

It provides a quick reference for all the key facts and concepts you need to understand as part of your exam preparation.

This pocket guide is fully aligned with the ITIL 2011 core volumes.

ABOUT THE AUTHOR

Claire Agutter has been an ITIL principal lecturer since 2007. She has been involved in exam panels for ITIL V2 and V3, and provides online ITIL training through IT Training Zone Ltd.

After training hundreds of successful Foundation delegates, she has condensed ITIL's key concepts into this pocket guide.

ACKNOWLEDGEMENTS

We would like to acknowledge the following reviewers of this book for their useful contributions: Kevin Holland, NHS; Suzanne D. Van Hove, Ed.D, FSM®, SED-IT, CEO & Founder; and Dave Jones, Pink Elephant.

CONTENTS

INTRODUCTION

Welcome to *ITIL Foundation Essentials*. This guide distils the key facts that you need to prepare for a successful ITIL Foundation exam.

This pocket guide is a great revision aid for anyone preparing for their Foundation exam, and is fully aligned with the latest syllabus and ITIL 2011 core volumes.

CHAPTER 1: INTRODUCING ITIL

ITIL is:

- Best practice for IT service management
- Developed by the UK government
- Globally adopted in the public and private sectors
- Not prescriptive
- A framework that organisations adopt and adapt.

Best practice is *"proven activities or processes that have been successfully used in multiple organisations"*. Best practice available in the public domain supports organisational improvement. Sources include public frameworks (ITIL) and standards like ISO/IEC 20000.

ITIL is successful because it's:

- Vendor neutral
- Non-prescriptive
- Best practice.

ITIL is preferable to proprietary information held within organisations, which may not be documented, challenged or improved.

Figure 1 shows the many sources of service management practice. Best practice must be passed through a filter of the drivers and scenarios relevant to the organisation before it is fit for purpose.

© Crown Copyright 2011 Cabinet Office.

Figure 1: Sources of service management best practice

CHAPTER 2: SERVICES

"A service is a means of delivering value to customers by facilitating outcomes customers want to achieve without the ownership of specific costs and risks."

For example, a customer using a data centre service does not want to take ownership of the costs of individual hardware elements, or manage risks related to power, etc. The customer wants to pay for, and use, the service.

IT service:

- Provided by IT service providers
    - Made up of IT, people and processes
    - Customer-facing IT services directly support the business processes of customer(s), according to SLA targets
    - Supporting services are used to deliver customer-facing services.

Service providers define results-based services focused on customer outcomes.

Outcome:

"The result of carrying out an activity, following a process or delivering an IT service. Outcome can refer to intended or actual results."

Customer expectations change. Service providers must update services so that they continue to deliver value.

Service classifications

- **Core services:** deliver basic outcomes desired by customer(s). They represent what the customer wants and will pay for. For example: e-mail.

- **Enabling services:** Required for the core service to be delivered. For example: the network used to access e-mail.

- **Enhancing services:** Non-essential services are added to the core service to tempt or excite customers. For example: mobile e-mail may be an optional extra.

Service providers use **service packages** to help organise services for customers. Service packages combine core, enabling and enhancing services. The package contains two or more services bundled together to meet customers' needs.

Service providers can be:

- **Type 1 or Internal:** has a one-to-one relationship with a business unit it provides services to, often embedded in the unit.

- **Type 2 or Shared Service Unit:** has a one-to-many relationship with internal business units.

- **Type 3 or External:** provides IT services to external customers.

Internal and external services

Internal services are delivered to departments or business units in the same organisation as the service provider. They support internal activity.

External services are delivered to an external customer, who could be an individual or another organisation. They support business outcomes.

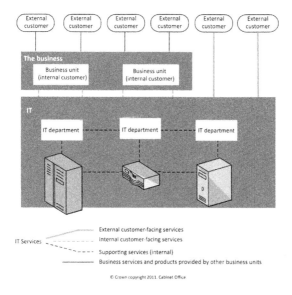

© Crown copyright 2011. Cabinet Office

Figure 2: Internal and external services

Types of service

- Supporting services:
o Often infrastructure services
o Required for other services to be delivered
o Customers may not be aware of them

- Internal customer-facing services
o Used by customers in the same organisation as the service provider

- External customer-facing services
o Customers are from different organisations.

CHAPTER 3: SERVICE MANAGEMENT

"A set of specialised organisational capabilities for delivering value to customers in the form of services."

Service management can include, for example, the staff skills and processes used to manage and support IT services.

Organisations develop service management capabilities and skills to respond to challenges including:

- The intangible nature of the output of a service process
- Customer assets that drive demand. Service providers have to balance supply and the cost of delivery
- Service provider and consumer have a high level of contact, often informal and not managed
- Service output is perishable and cannot be stockpiled.

Service management as a professional practice

Service management is supported by knowledge, experience and skills that have built up as the IT industry developed a service focus.

A global community of professionals supports service management, including the IT Service Management Forum (*www.itsmfi.org*).

Service management is also supported by a scheme that provides education, training and certification. Available service management information includes academic research and standards, such as ISO/IEC 20000.

IT service management

"The implementation and management of quality IT services that meet the needs of the business. IT service management is performed by IT service providers through an appropriate mix of people, process and information technology."

IT organisations must understand customer requirements. Service providers use service management to deliver customer outcomes, and need to be efficient and effective, delivering high quality IT services.

Service providers balance three areas:

- Customer needs
- Service performance
- Customer budget.

CHAPTER 4: STAKEHOLDERS

"... any person who has an interest in an organisation, project, IT service or other area. Stakeholders may be interested in activities, targets, resources or deliverables."

Examples of stakeholders are customers, partners, employees, shareholders, owners.

IT must understand internal and external stakeholders. Internal stakeholders are from the same organisation as the service provider.

External stakeholders are from a different organisation.

Stakeholders include:

- **Customers:** buy goods or services/define what services must do
- **Users:** use services regularly
- **Suppliers:** third parties, supply goods or services that form all or part of services.

Customers divide into two groups:

- Internal customers from the same organisation
- External customers from a different organisation.

Service providers must meet customers' expectations.

There are differences between internal and external customers, including:

- **Funding:** how the service is paid for
- **Business strategy and objectives:** do the customer and service provider share objectives?

- **Accounting:** how important is service price?
- **Involvement with Service Design, Transition, Operation and Improvement:** internal customers may have more involvement.

CHAPTER 5: PROCESSES, FUNCTIONS, ROLES

Processes

"... a structured set of activities designed to accomplish a specific objective. A process takes one or more defined inputs and turns them into defined outputs."

Processes are closed loop systems that request feedback and use it to improve performance.

Process models

These are used to design and map processes. Processes need to be documented so they can be shared.

Figure 3 shows the main elements of a process model. This needs to include the inputs and outputs, the resources required, and how the process is measured and managed.

Process characteristics

- Respond to triggers
- Deliver a result
- Deliver value to a customer/stakeholder
- Measurable.

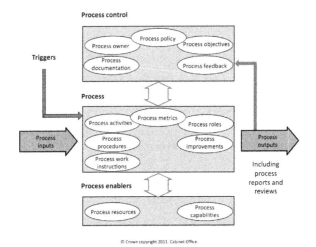

© Crown copyright 2011. Cabinet Office.

Figure 3: The process model

Functions

"A team or group of people and the tools or other resources they use to carry out one or more processes or activities."

Common IT functions include the Service Desk and technical support teams.

Roles

"A set of responsibilities, activities and authorities granted to a person or team. A role is defined in a process or function. One person or team can have multiple roles."

A single person can fulfil many roles. For example, a Service Desk team member may carry out roles related to Incident Management, Request Fulfilment and Access Management.

Job descriptions for staff will outline the roles they need to fulfil.

CHAPTER 6: THE SERVICE LIFECYCLE

- Five stages documented in five volumes, forming the ITIL core
- Service Strategy, Service Design, Service Transition, Service Operation and Continual Service Improvement
- Tracks a service from inception to retirement
- Service Strategy is the hub that drives the lifecycle
- CSI looks for improvements in all stages.

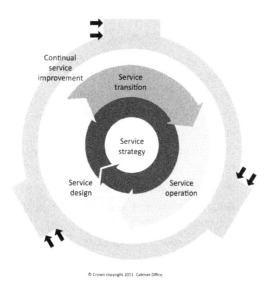

© Crown copyright 2011. Cabinet Office.

Figure 4: The service lifecycle

The core is supplemented by complementary guidance, specific to industry sectors, organisation types, operating models and technology architectures.

Service Strategy

Purpose and objectives

To define:

- What a service provider needs to do to support its customer
- A strategy to support business outcomes
- Plans, patterns, position and perspective for service provider behaviour.

Objectives include understanding:

- What strategy is, what services are, who customers are
- How value is created and delivered
- The service provision model for how services are delivered and funded
- Opportunities to offer services and how to act on them
- If the organisation can deliver the strategy
- What service assets make up services and how they are managed
- What processes need to exist for the strategy to be delivered.

Service assets
Any resource or capability of a service provider. Services are made up of service assets, including people, hardware, software, etc. Service providers manage and optimise assets.

Table 1: Service assets

The diagram below shows examples of capabilities and resources. Resources are direct inputs to production and easily acquired; capabilities are harder to acquire and based on experience of contracts, customers, people, tools and processes.

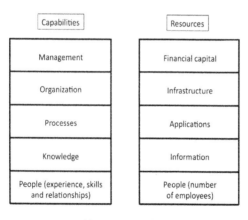

© Crown copyright 2011. Cabinet Office

Figure 5: Examples of capabilities and resources

Scope

This includes defining principles and processes for service management which then apply to the rest of the service lifecycle. IT service providers need a coherent strategy to ensure their services deliver value.

The scope covers two areas:

- Defining a strategy for how the service provider will deliver services to meet customer needs
- Defining a strategy for ongoing service management.

Value

Service Strategy helps organisations to:

- Offer services and meet business needs in a timely way
- Link IT activities and assets to business outcomes
- Demonstrate return on IT investment
- Be a trusted partner.

Service Design

Purpose and Objectives

- Design services to underpin strategy
- Design IT processes, practices, policies
- Ensure services are high quality, cost effective, meet customer needs.

Effective design reduces the total cost of ownership of a service and leads to less rework later in the lifecycle.

Scope

- Design of appropriate, innovative services
- Meet current and future customer needs
- Influenced by requirements, business benefits, constraints.

Value

Service Design helps organisations to improve:

- Service quality, implementation consistency and performance
- Governance and decision making
- Service management and processes
- Optimisation of service cost.

Service Transition

Purpose and objectives

Service Transition ensures new, modified or retired services meet business expectations documented during Service Strategy and Design.

Objectives include:

- Manage service changes efficiently and effectively
- Manage change-related risks
- Deploy releases successfully
- Set expectations about service performance and use
- Ensure changes create value

- Provide knowledge and information about services and service assets
- Introduce a framework to manage changes and protect assets
- Use repeatable processes.

Scope

Service Transition is responsible for developing and improving capabilities for getting new and changed services into the live environment.

Processes need to be in place for release build, test and deployment to ensure changes meet objectives, without creating unnecessary problems.

The scope also includes retirement of services and movement of services between providers.

Service Transition uses seven processes:

- Change Management, Service Asset and Configuration Management, and Knowledge Management: involved in the whole service lifecycle.
- Transition Planning and Support, Release and Deployment Management, Service Validation and Testing, and Change Evaluation: only operate within Service Transition.

Value

Service Transition helps organisations to:

- Deliver successful changes
- Improve communication, expectation setting and confidence in changes

- Reduce costs, delays and timing issues
- Improve control of service assets and configuration items.

Service Operation

Purpose and Objectives

- Undertakes activities and processes to manage and deliver services at agreed levels
- Manages technology
- Collects information on service performance.

Objectives include:

- Maintain business confidence and satisfaction with service delivery
- Minimise the business effect of down time
- Allow only authorised users to have service access.

Scope

This includes every element of service delivery:

- Services
- Service management processes
- Technology
- People.

Value

Service Operation helps organisations to:

- Reduce outage frequency and impact

- Provide access to standard services
- Provide data to justify investment.

Continual Service Improvement (CSI)

Purpose and objectives

CSI interacts with all lifecycle phases. It identifies improvements to align services with changing business needs.

Organisations must embed a culture of improvement in everything they do.

Objectives include:

- Review, analyse and prioritise improvements across the whole lifecycle
- Review service target performance
- Identify and implement improvement activities
- Improve cost effectiveness without affecting performance
- Use quality management methodologies
- Ensure processes have objectives and measures
- Understand what to measure and why.

Scope

CSI scope includes:

- The health of IT service management
- Alignment of services to current and future business needs
- Maturity and capability of the organisation, management, processes and people

- Continual improvement of IT services and service assets.

Value

CSI helps organisations to:

- Improve quality and reduce cost
- Align services to business requirements
- Improve services, structure, processes, capabilities and communication.

CHAPTER 7: SERVICE STRATEGY

Concept: Value creation

Customers must understand service value.

- Value is defined by the customer – not the provider
- An affordable mix of features needs to be on offer for the customer to want a service
- Value might not be measured in financial terms alone – the customer might value a service because it fulfils an ethical or moral objective
- Value changes over time.

The customer must see service value as outweighing service cost. IT needs to articulate what:

- Services it provides
- The services achieve
- The services cost.

Figure 6 shows the components of value.

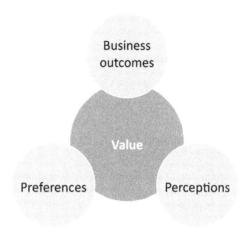

Figure 6: Components of value

Value is influenced by:

- Outcomes achieved – does the service support the customer as intended?
- Customer preferences – how do these affect the service?
- Customer perceptions – are these influenced by any other areas, such as supplier reputation?

Some services have financial value linked to business outcomes. Services that support internal activity might not directly influence revenue.

Figure 7 shows how customers perceive the value a service delivers. Customers start with a reference value for a service. Positive and negative differences achieved by using the service give a net difference – the service's economic value.

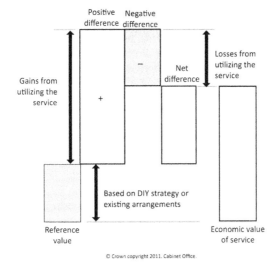

© Crown copyright 2011. Cabinet Office.

Figure 7: How customers perceive value

Concept: Utility and warranty

Utility and warranty measure value.

- Utility: fit for purpose, has required functionality, enhances performance or removes constraints
- Warranty: fit for use, includes availability, continuity, security, capacity.

Utility and warranty must both be offered for a service to deliver value.

Utility is what is delivered; warranty is how it is delivered. For example, internet banking utility could include the ability to pay bills online. Warranty could include confidence that information is secure.

Concept: Risk management

Risk: "*a possible event that could cause harm or loss, or affect the ability to achieve objectives*".

Risk management needs to be embedded in service management.

- Stage 1: identify risks. Document and analyse them.
- Stage 2: manage risks. Based on priority, action plans will be documented and reviewed.

Concept: Governance

Governance defines common directions, policies and rules for the business and IT. IT must work within any existing governance structure.

Governance:

- Ensures policies and strategy are implemented, and processes are followed.
- Defines roles and responsibilities, measures and reports. It instigates actions to resolve any issues.

Effective governance leads to consistency at all organisational levels. Strategies feed into policies, which feed into plans and ways of working.

Concept: Patterns of Business Activity (PBA)

A PBA is *"a workload profile of one or more business activities. PBAs are used to help the IT service provider understand and plan for different levels of business activity".*

PBAs reflect changing customer use of services. They need to be identified, documented and change controlled to ensure services support customer demand.

Customer demand can be difficult to predict, but not impossible. It can be influenced, for example, by peak and off-peak charging.

PBA definitions need to include:

- Classification: type of PBA and workload
- Attributes: volume, frequency, location, duration
- Requirements: e.g. performance, availability
- Service asset requirements: what is needed to fulfil demand?

Service Strategy processes

Service Portfolio Management

Purpose and objectives

- Ensures the service provider has the right mix of services to meet customer requirements
- Tracks investment and return
- Defines services and links them to business outcomes, influencing the service lifecycle.

Objectives:

- Provides a process and mechanism to help the service provider decide what services to provide
- Maintains a definitive portfolio of services
- Provides a mechanism to show how services will support organisational strategy
- Controls which services are offered and when
- Tracks investment in services
- Analyses which services should be retired and when.

Scope

- Includes all services
- Ensures the service provider can deliver value through services
- Services are linked to business outcomes so investment can be compared to returns
- Newer services need to add more value than the services they replace.

Concept: Service Portfolio

Service Portfolio: the full set of services managed by a service provider, including:

- Proposed or in development
- Live
- Retired.

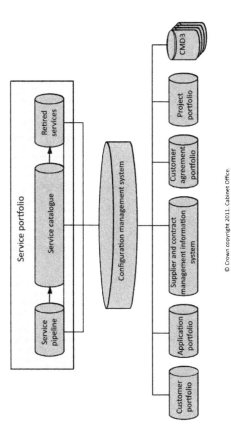

© Crown copyright 2011. Cabinet Office.

Figure 8: The service portfolio

Only services that add value are included in the portfolio.

- **Service pipeline:** services that are being developed – not normally visible to customers
- **Service catalogue:** services that are live, visible to customers
- **Retired services:** services may be retired when they are no longer offered to new customers, or when they are no longer offered to any customers. This is typically because they are no longer useful or profitable.

Third-party services may also be included in the portfolio.

Financial Management for IT Services (FMITS)

Purpose and objectives

- Secure funding for service design, development and delivery
- Balance cost and quality
- Implement a framework to identify, manage and communicate service costs
- Evaluate the financial impact of new or changed strategies.

Most organisations have a business Financial Management process. FMITS needs specialised skills. Practitioners need to understand technology, as well as finance and business. Cost-accounting skills are required to provide detailed management information.

IT financial policies and practices need to follow organisational guidelines to allow IT and other business areas to communicate.

Scope

FMITS includes three processes:

- **Budgeting** predicts and controls income and expenditure
- **Accounting** tracks how money is spent
- **Charging** bills customers for services provided (may not apply to all service providers).

Accounting, budgeting and charging have two cycles of activity. On an annual basis, projections and plans are produced. Operationally, costs are monitored and checked, and bills are issued. This normally happens monthly or quarterly.

Concept: Business case

A business case is *"justification for a significant item of expenditure"*.

Business cases include:

- Introduction
- Methods, assumptions
- Business impacts of proposed action – financial and non-financial
- Risk and contingencies
- Recommendations.

Business cases are used to justify investment in new or changed services. They will be an input to processes including Service Portfolio Management and Change Management – as part of a change proposal.

Business Relationship Management (BRM)

Purpose and objectives

BRM will:

- Establish and maintain the customer/service provider relationship
- Identify current and future customer needs and make sure they are met.

Objectives include:

- Ensuring the service provider understands the customer perspective
- Improving customer satisfaction
- Identifying changes to the customer environment or technology that could affect services
- Establishing and communicating requirements for new or changed services
- Implementing a process to manage complaints.

Scope

Internal BRM usually happens at management level. External BRM may involve account managers or a dedicated Business Relationship Manager.

Internal providers try to meet business goals and objectives. External providers try to maximise contract value through satisfied customers.

BRM focuses on the customer, not individual services. It needs strong relationships with other service management processes, like Service Portfolio Management, to fulfil its role.

BRM and Service Level Management (SLM)

These processes are often confused.

BRM focuses on the customer relationship, SLM on services and targets. BRM will focus on required utility and warranty, and SLM will focus on the warranty agreed.

BRM is strategic and tactical, SLM is tactical and operational.

Each process is measured on its focus area.

CHAPTER 8: SERVICE DESIGN

IT processes, practices and policies need to be designed to make sure that services are high quality, cost effective, and meet customer needs.

Design makes sure customer expectations are met. Modern IT organisations are pressured to deliver solutions quickly. Good design becomes even more important.

Model: 4 Ps

The 4 Ps need to be considered together for successful service management.

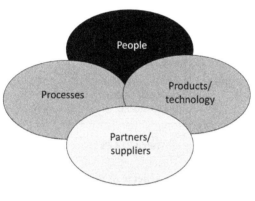

Figure 9: The 4 Ps

People	• Vital for ITIL initiatives, projects and enhancements • Need education and awareness, communication, expectation setting.
Processes	It's important to define: • Process objectives • Process documentation • KPIs and metrics that track process performance.
Products	Includes any tools or products that provide, manage or measure services.
Partners	Third-party impact on service delivery needs to be understood.

Table 2: 4 Ps

Concept: Five major aspects of Service Design

- Five areas where Service Design has objectives and activities
- Support a holistic design approach.

Aspect 1: Design of management information systems and tools

Includes the design of the Service Portfolio, used to ensure new or changed services are consistent with and interface with existing services.

Aspect 2: Design of service solutions

Includes establishing service requirements to support high-level decisions made in Service Strategy.

Detailed business requirements are needed to support design, including business needs, strategy, timescales and resources.

Aspect 3: Design of technology and management architecture

Technical architectures ensure new services fit with existing services and meet business needs.

They provide guidance on long-term technical direction to feed into design activities. This prevents resources being wasted on unapproved or unauthorised technologies.

Aspect 4: Design of processes

Processes are developed, documented and controlled to support new or changed services. Process owners, inputs, outputs, roles, responsibilities and skills are documented.

Aspect 5: Design of measurement methods and metrics

Measurements are used to demonstrate service value, addressing progress, compliance, efficiency, effectiveness.

New systems and metrics may be included or procured as part of a service.

Service Design processes

Service Level Management (SLM)

Purpose and objectives

- Ensures current and planned services are delivered to agreed, achievable targets
- Negotiates, agrees, monitors, reports and reviews IT service targets
- Takes corrective action if targets are not achieved
- Initiates service improvements.

Objectives include:

- Managing the agreement and review of targets and responsibilities documented in Service Level Agreements and Operational Level Agreements
- Working with BRM to improve customer relationships
- Making sure all IT services have targets in place
- Monitoring and improving customer satisfaction
- Making sure IT and the customer have a clear, unambiguous understanding of the level of service to be delivered
- Cost effectively improving service performance.

Scope

SLM is the bridge between IT and the business. The process needs to be neutral.

SLM looks at current and future services, collecting and documenting realistic customer requirements.

During Service Design, SLM makes sure all services have targets and will not negatively affect live services.

Excluded from the SLM scope:

- Agreeing detailed functionality requirements
- Carrying out technical activities
- Negotiating supplier contracts.

Concept: Service Level Agreement (SLA)

"An agreement between an IT service provider and a customer."

- Documents service targets agreed with the customer
- Describes the service, targets, reports and reporting cycle
  - Reviewed regularly for relevance.

Concept: Operational Level Agreement (OLA)

"An agreement between an IT service provider and another part of the same organization. It supports the IT service provider's delivery of IT services to customers and defines the goods or services to be provided and the responsibilities of both parties. For example, there could be an operational level agreement between the IT service provider and a procurement department to obtain hardware in agreed times."

Concept: Contract

"A legally binding agreement between 2 or more parties."

- Documents third-party service delivery elements
- May be referred to as 'underpinning contract'
- Managed by Supplier Management.

Concept: Service Level Requirements (SLRs)

"A customer requirement for an aspect of an IT service. SLRs are based on business objectives and used to negotiate agreed service level targets."

- Collected from customers and documented by SLM early in the design process
- Aligned to service criticality
- Need to be based on what IT can actually do – input required from Capacity and Availability Management.

Concept: Types of SLA

Three types of SLA can be used depending on the type of service and organisation:

- **Service-based:** covers one service, and is applied to all customers of that service. For example, the e-mail service for all business departments
- **Customer-based:** for a single customer, covering all of the services that they use. For example, the Finance Department agreement

might cover the e-mail, payroll and invoicing services

- **Multi-level SLAs:** implemented with a layered structure to cover different needs – such as corporate, customer and service layers. For example, service hours and support might be agreed at the corporate level. One customer with specific needs might have longer service hours agreed, and for a specific service might have 24x7 support.

The Service Level Manager has to decide which will be most appropriate. All SLAs must be clear, concise and unambiguous. Targets cannot be included if they cannot be measured.

Concept: SLA Monitoring Chart (SLAM Chart)

- Often colour-coded, so customers can see targets met/missed
- May be based around a traffic light system – red: target missed; amber: near miss; green: target met
- Feed into service review meetings.

Concept: Service review

- Held regularly (often monthly)
- Attended by SLM and the customer
- Agenda includes service performance and changes to requirements
- Output is fed into Service Improvement Plans (SIPs).

Concept: Service Improvement Plan

"A formal plan to implement improvements to a process or IT service."

SLM Activities

These include:

- Working with customers to agree SLRs and SLAs
- Measuring service performance against SLA targets
- Producing service reports and conducting service reviews
- Working with CSI and managing Service Improvement Plans (SIPs) for the implementation of service or process improvements
- Working with BRM to measure and improve customer satisfaction
- Review and revision of SLAs, service scope and OLAs
- Supporting Supplier Management
- Developing business contacts and managing complaints and compliments
- Providing management information.

Service Catalogue Management

Purpose and objectives

Provides a single source of information on operational services, and those about to become operational.

Service Catalogues describe live services and need to be available to users and any relevant stakeholders.

Objectives include:

- Manage information in the Service Catalogue and make sure it's accurate
- Make the catalogue available and useful
- Ensure the catalogue supports other service management processes.

Scope

The process will create a definition of 'service' and help to define service packages. The catalogue needs to be populated before it can be released.

Concept: Service Catalogue Structure

There are two main types of structure, used to provide information to customers.

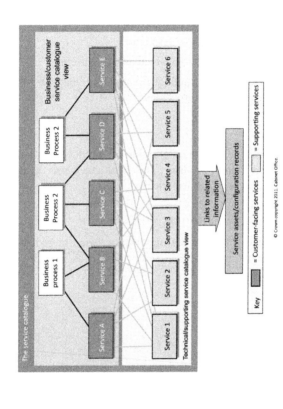

Figure 10: A two view service catalogue

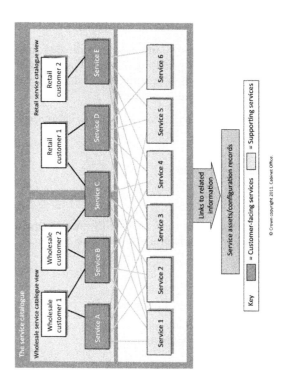

Figure 11: A three view service catalogue

Two view catalogue: shows information relevant to customers while protecting them from technical and supporting services which could create confusion. For example, customers might see an e-mail service, but not the back-up and network services that support e-mail.

Three view catalogue: customers are divided into segments and shown targeted information. For example, the retail customers will have different services offered to them than the wholesale customers.

Each organisation needs to adopt an appropriate structure.

Availability Management

Purpose and objectives

Ensures the level of service availability meets agreed targets or customer needs in a cost-effective and timely manner.

Objectives include:

- Meet current and future business needs
- Produce an availability plan (normally annual) to outline investment requirements
- Advise the business and other IT teams
- Make sure availability targets are met
- Advise on availability incidents and impact of changes
    - Identify proactive measures to improve availability and implement where cost justified.

Scope

The process starts when availability requirements are clear and finishes at service retirement. It includes the design, implementation, measurement, management and improvement of IT service and component availability.

The scope also includes:

- Reactive activities – such as involvement with incident management
- Proactive activities – designing availability into services.

Availability Management should be applied to all services and needs to understand business and IT information.

The process will:

- Measure availability
- Report at service and component levels
- Use component resilience to build high availability services where needed
- Store availability information in the Availability Management Information System.

Concept: Availability measures

Availability

"Ability of an IT service or other configuration item to perform its agreed function when required."

- Defined as a service or IT component being available when needed
- Usually calculated as a percentage
- Normally measured during Agreed Service Time (AST). Down time outside normal service hours will not have the same impact on the user
- The higher the availability required, the greater the cost of service provision.

Reliability

"A measure of how long an IT service or other configuration item can perform its agreed function without interruption."

- Services that are infrequently unavailable are reliable
- Often measured as the Mean Time Between Failures (MTBF).

Maintainability

"A measure of how quickly and effectively an IT service or other configuration item can be restored to normal working after a failure."

- Measured as Mean Time to Restore Service (MTRS).

Serviceability

"The ability of a third party supplier to meet the terms of its contract. This contract will include agreed levels of reliability, availability and maintainability for a configuration item."

Concept: Vital Business Function (VBF)

A VBF defines the critical part of a business process. For example, an ATM dispenses cash and statements. Dispensing cash could be described as a VBF, but statements aren't as essential.

Resources and protection are targeted towards critical service elements.

Concept: Service and Component Availability

Availability Management needs to measure and manage at service and component levels.

- *"Service availability: involves all aspects of service availability and unavailability and the impact of component availability, or unavailability on service availability"*

- *"Component availability: involves all aspects of component availability and unavailability".*

Information Security Management (ISM)

Purpose and objectives

Responsible for aligning IT security with the business security policy and ensuring that security is designed into services and service management activities.

ISM sets standards that need to be available to everyone in the business. Security is part of the service **warranty**.

ISM objectives relate to protection of information and people who use information. The security objective is met when information:

- **Is confidential:** only accessed by those who have the right to see it

- **Has integrity:** complete, accurate and protected from unapproved change

- **Is available and usable when needed:** information can resist and recover from attacks or failures

- **Has authenticity and non-repudiation:** information shared between organisations or partners can be trusted.

Scope

ISM is the focal point for security issues. It produces a security policy that links to business policies and legislative requirements.

ISM ensures security is designed into services.

The process manages security breaches and organises reviews and tests.

Concept: Information Security Policy

Organisations need an overall Information Security Policy to direct security activity. The policy needs to have management support and be available to everyone who needs it.

The policy will address areas such as password control, anti-virus and asset disposal.

Supplier Management

Purpose and objectives

This process is responsible for managing external suppliers and the services they supply. This results in quality IT services that are good value for money.

Supplier Management is responsible for managing the lifecycle of a supplier relationship, including choosing a supplier, getting the right contract and supplier negotiation.

Suppliers are monitored in line with the organisational supplier policy. At contract end, the termination or renegotiation process needs to be managed.

Supplier Categorisation

Suppliers are categorised based on risk, impact, value and importance. More effort and resources is dedicated to managing important suppliers.

- **Strategic:**
  o Relevant for significant partnering relationships that involve senior managers sharing confidential strategic information to facilitate long-term plans
  o Normally managed and owned by senior management

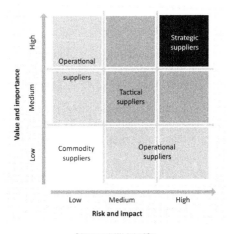

Figure 12: Supplier categorisation

- **Tactical:**
  o Relevant for relationships involving significant commercial activity and business interaction
  o Normally managed by middle management

- **Operational:**
  o Used for suppliers of operational products or services
  o Normally managed by junior operational management

- **Commodity:**
  o Suppliers that provide low-value and/or readily available products and services
  o Could be alternatively sourced relatively easily.

Capacity Management

Purpose and objectives

This process ensures the capacity of IT services and infrastructure meets business needs in a cost-effective and timely way.

It plans ahead to make sure new services don't have capacity issues.

Capacity Management measures, maintains and improves service performance; it balances cost against resources, and supply against demand.

Objectives include:

- Produce a capacity plan
- Advise the business and IT
- Make sure capacity issues do not affect service
- Carry out reactive activities including working with incident management
- Carry out proactive activities, e.g. change impact assessment and implementation of improvements.

Scope

The process will:

- Be a focal point for capacity information
- Track capacity of hardware, software, infrastructure and people
- Work with Service Strategy to understand long-term business needs
- Carry out monitoring

- Tune and refine services and infrastructure to optimise performance
- Influence demand to offset investment
- Track technology improvements that could affect capacity.

Capacity Management sub-processes

- **Business Capacity Management:** strategic, uses future business plans to assess impact on capacity and helps to translate business plans and needs into requirements
- **Service Capacity Management:** tactical, manages, controls and predicts end-to-end service performance to make sure targets can be met
- **Component Capacity Management:** operational, manages, controls and predicts component performance, utilisation and capacity, using automation where possible.

Concept: Capacity plan

Capacity Management produces the capacity plan, which includes:

- Current and historic use of IT services and components
- Any issues or improvement activities
- Scenarios for levels of business demand
- Investment required to meet service targets, including costed options.

IT Service Continuity Management (ITSCM)

Purpose and objectives

ITSCM supports Business Continuity Management. It manages risk and plans for service recovery in the event of a disaster.

Business Continuity Plans provide information about how quickly services need to be recovered.

Objectives include:

- Maintaining IT Service Continuity and IT recovery plans – these need to be updated and regularly assessed
- Carrying out regular business impact analysis exercises, to track the changing criticality of business services
- Carrying out risk analysis and management, providing advice and guidance as needed
- Assessing the impact of changes on the plans
- Negotiating contracts with suppliers who provide services that support plans.

Scope

Anything deemed a disaster is in scope. The more complex the service, the more complex the ITSC planning required.

Long-term business changes are not in scope, e.g. an organisational restructure would be handled at the strategic level.

ITSCM has a four-step process:

- **Initiation:** driven by BCM
- **Requirements and strategy:** carrying out business impact analysis and risk assessment
- **Implementation:** producing plans and implementing risk reduction measures
- **Ongoing operation:** including regular testing of the plans.

Concept: Business Impact Analysis (BIA)

This technique determines the financial and non-financial effect of service loss.

The output is usually a graph showing escalation over time. It's used to identify minimum staffing and infrastructure levels to maintain a service. This guides ITSCM effort and investment.

BIA helps to determine recovery requirements and recovery times.

Concept: Risk assessment

Identifies the level of threat and how vulnerable an organisation is. Used to identify what to protect and how much to invest by ITSCM, Availability and Information Security Management.

Standard methodologies like Management of Risk (M_o_R[®2]) may be used. Countermeasures are used to reduce risks where appropriate.

Risk assessment helps to determine risk responses and risk reduction, based on a risk profile.

---

[2] *http://www.mor-officialsite.com/.*

Design Co-ordination

Purpose and objectives

This process co-ordinates all Service Design processes and activities to make sure they work consistently.

It will:

- Co-ordinate resources
- Hand plans (including the Service Design Package) to Service Transition in a timely way
- Make sure designs conform to corporate requirements
- Identify improvements to Service Design effectiveness and efficiency
- Provide a common framework of reusable practices.

Scope

The process covers all design activities. Complex designs require more co-ordination.

The process will:

- Assist and support projects
- Co-ordinate, prioritise and schedule activities
- Review, measure and improve activities.

The process will only **co-ordinate** activities within Service Design – it does not carry them out.

Concept: Service Design Package (SDP)

The SDP is handed to Service Transition in an agreed format when design is complete. Design Co-ordination is responsible for the production of SDP.

It includes *"documents defining all aspects of an IT service and its requirements through each stage of its lifecycle. An SDP is produced for each new IT service, major change or service retirement."*

The SDP includes information for Transition, Operation and CSI including:

- Requirements
- Service Design
- Metrics
- Organisational readiness assessment
- Requirements for new or changed processes
- Service lifecycle plan – including definition for transition and operation
- Service Acceptance Criteria.

CHAPTER 9: SERVICE TRANSITION

Service Transition processes

Change Management

Purpose and objectives

This process controls the lifecycle of changes. Service providers need to transition new or changed services into the production environment smoothly.

Objectives include:

- Responding to changing business requirements while minimising disruption
- Managing and implementing changes to align services with business needs
- Recording and managing changes
- Optimising change-related business risk.

Scope

Management of all changes across the service lifecycle, including changes to physical and virtual assets.

The scope includes changes to the five aspects of Service Design.

Figure 13 shows the scope of Change Management.

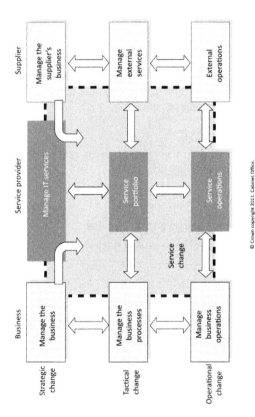

© Crown copyright 2011. Cabinet Office.

Figure 13: Scope of Change Management

Sources of change include:

- Service Strategy and Service Portfolio Management for strategic changes
- Service Design, CSI, SLM and Service Catalogue Management for service changes
- Service Operation for corrective changes.

Not in scope:

- Business changes: managed by business change management with support from IT where required
- Co-ordination of service management processes during a change.

Concept: Change

Adding, modifying or removing anything that could affect IT services. This includes changes to architectures, processes, tools, metrics, documentation, CIs and services.

Concept: Change Proposal

"A document that includes a high level description of a potential service introduction or significant change, along with a corresponding business case and expected implementation schedule."

- Normally created by Service Portfolio Management
- Authorised by Change Management
- Describes a possible service introduction or change at a high level

- Normally used for significant (high cost, risk or impact) changes
- Produced for impact analysis and approval before a service is chartered
- The effect on existing services needs to be considered.

Approved proposals are passed back to Service Portfolio Management who may then create requests for change for individual pieces of work.

Concept: Change Request

A change request is a formal communication requesting change to one or more CIs, such as a Service Desk call, project document, Request for Change or Change Proposal.

Templates are used to capture information.

Types of change

The level of management applied to a change depends on the associated risk and impact.

There are three main types of change:

- **Standard change:** low risk and impact, a pre-authorised approach has been agreed with Change Management. Authority for these changes can be delegated, e.g. to the Service Desk Manager. They must have a defined trigger, be low risk and have a proven, documented procedure.
- **Normal change:** higher risk, normally requested by a change initiator. Need to be

assessed by stakeholders before implementation.

- **Emergency change:** used to respond to major incidents or critical service failures. Need to be designed, managed and tested as far as possible, but may be recorded retrospectively.

Changes may also be categorised as major, significant and minor. The categorisation will depend on the level of risk associated with the change.

Concept: Change Model

Models document steps to provide a repeatable way of carrying out a change. Models should be automated to improve consistency.

They include:

- Steps to be taken
- Timescales, thresholds and chronological order for completion of activities
- Roles and responsibilities
- Escalation points and procedures
- Dependencies.

Example process flow for a normal Change Model:

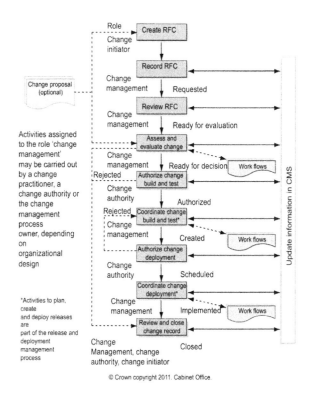

© Crown copyright 2011. Cabinet Office.

Figure 14: Example of a process flow for a normal change

RFC Step	Notes
Create	• Change initiator creates RFC • Includes business case or business approvals.
Record	In a tool or using manual documents.
Review	Change Management checks all information is present and accepts the change.
Assess and evaluate	May include consultation with stakeholders including CAB members.
Authorise change build and test	Approval is given to allocate resources and carry out build/test activities.
Co-ordinate change build and test	Change Management monitors progress and checks the change will perform as required. They don't carry out the activities.

Authorise deployment	This will happen if the build and test have been successful.
Co-ordinate deployment	Monitors for anything unusual.
Review and close	Changes are reviewed against their original objectives. The review also ensures the change process is working.

Table 3: Request for Change steps

Concept: Remediation Planning

All changes must have a remediation plan, referenced in the implementation plan. Remediation includes *"actions taken to recover after a failed change or release. This could include back-out, invocation of ITSC plans, or other actions ... to enable the business process to continue."*

Concept: Change Advisory Board (CAB)

The CAB is the group of stakeholders who support Change Management in the assessment, prioritisation and scheduling of changes.

Membership will vary according to the changes being discussed, and include customers, users, developers, third parties, etc.

CAB members will:

- Review and approve normal changes
- Periodically review standard changes
- Review emergency changes post-implementation.

If a decision cannot be reached at CAB, a change may be escalated to senior management.

A standard CAB agenda would include the review of:

- Failed, unauthorised and backed-out changes
- New requests
- Emergency and standard changes
- The Change Management process.

In an emergency, it may not be possible to convene a CAB. A subset of the CAB – the Emergency Change Advisory Board or ECAB – meets instead to make a quick decision.

Emergency changes must still be recorded.

Interfaces

Change Management needs good relationships within IT and with the business. Changes will not be raised if the process is not visible.

Interfaces include:

- Business Change Management: business change might drive IT change
- Programme and Project Management: Change Management needs early involvement
- Organisational and Stakeholder Change Management: changes might affect staff or organisational structure

- Sourcing and Partnering: change management needs to integrate with internal and external vendors and partners

- Service Asset and Configuration Management: supports impact assessment

- Problem Management: raises changes and contributes at CAB

- ITSCM: changes need to be assessed for their impact on IT service continuity

- Information Security Management: changes need to be assessed for their impact on security

- Capacity and Demand Management: changes need to be assessed for their impact on capacity and demand, and Capacity Management may raise changes

- Service Portfolio Management: submits change proposals and may contribute to change assessment.

Service Asset and Configuration Management (SACM)

Purpose and objectives

- To control assets used to deliver services

- To provide information – where assets are and their use.

The process tracks Configuration Items (CIs) and relationships between them, including hardware, software, people, documents and buildings.

Current, historical and planned environments can be understood.

SACM will:

- Manage CIs by identifying, controlling, recording, reporting, auditing and verifying them during their lifecycle

- Protect assets and services

- Work with Change Management to ensure authorised assets are used

- Keep accurate information about CIs.

Scope

SACM manages CIs. All CIs are service assets, but not all service assets are CIs: for example, staff experience is a service asset that cannot be managed as a CI.

SACM identifies CIs, usually via an automated tool. It will use information to create a configuration model showing how CIs deliver a service. Non-IT assets will be included where relevant.

If an asset management process exists, SACM may use this as an information source.

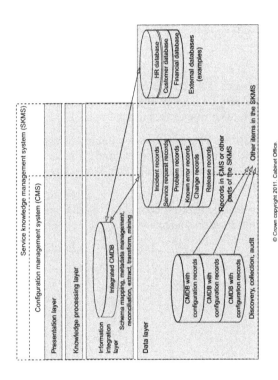

Figure 15: Example of the application of the architectural layers of the CMS

© Crown copyright 2011. Cabinet Office.

Concept: Configuration Management System (CMS)

For each CI, SACM stores attributes, e.g. purchase date, model, unique identifier, SLA, related changes, incidents, etc.

The process organises data and records in the CMS, which forms part of an overall Service Knowledge Management System.

Figure 15 shows the different layers of the CMS.

CMS levels:

- **Data:** includes configuration records, may be stored in Configuration Management Databases (CMDB)
- **Integration:** aggregates information
- **Processing:** queries data
- **Presentation:** delivers information.

Technology may be based around a single data store or links between stores as appropriate.

Concept: Configuration baselines

A baseline is the reviewed and agreed normal state of a product, service or infrastructure. Once agreed, change must be authorised.

Baselines are used to:

- Mark a development milestone
- Build a service to an agreed state
- Change or rebuild a service
- Collect relevant components before build
- Develop a back-out plan.

Concept: Snapshot

A snapshot is a picture of a CI's or service's current state at a specific point in time. This may be unauthorised. They show what needs to be done to restore the baseline.

They can be stored as historical records or 'footprints'.

Concept: Definitive Media Library and Definitive Spares

DML: *"one or more locations in which definitive and authorised versions of all software configuration items are securely stored. The DML may also contain associated CIs such as licenses and documentation. It is a single logical storage area..."*

Definitive spares: *"an area ... set aside for the secure storage of definitive hardware spares".*

The DML and definitive spares make sure that physical CIs are secure and controlled.

Figure 16 shows the relationship between the DML and the CMS.

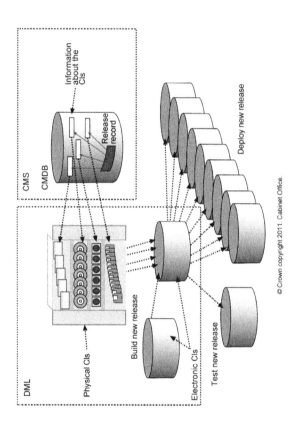

© Crown copyright 2011. Cabinet Office.

Figure 16: The relationship between the definitive media library and the CMS

Controlling physical assets means:

- Correct versions are used
- Licences are tracked
- Illegal software is identified.

Knowledge Management

Purpose and objectives

Knowledge Management shares perspectives, ideas, experience and information. Organisations are more efficient if information is available to the right person at the right time, and doesn't need to be rediscovered.

Objectives include:

- Improve decision making
- Improve service quality and reduce cost by making information available when needed
- Ensure staff understand how services deliver value
- Manage and maintain knowledge, information and data
- Maintain a Service Knowledge Management System (SKMS) to provide access to information.

Scope

Knowledge Management is a lifecycle-wide process that helps many other service management processes. It has a strong relationship with SACM, as the CMS helps to inform the overall SKMS.

Knowledge Management is not responsible for capturing and managing configuration data – this is the role of SACM.

Concept: Data Information Knowledge Wisdom Model (DIKW)

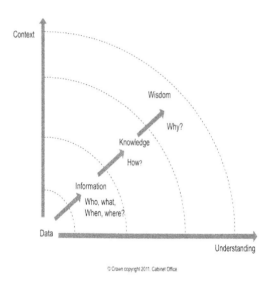

© Crown copyright 2011. Cabinet Office

Figure 17: The flow from data to wisdom

Knowledge Management is often displayed using this model.

Data: a set of discrete facts about events

- Large amounts may be captured in databases

- Data is often unformatted
- Too much data makes key facts hard to identify.

Information: provides context to data

- Typically stored in a semi-structured fashion
- Needs to be managed to facilitate capture, query, search and reuse
- Allows organisations to learn from experience.

Knowledge: includes information and the tacit experiences, ideas, insights, values and the judgements of individuals.

People gain knowledge from individual expertise and the analysis of information and data. By combining the skills and knowledge of individuals with available data and information, knowledge is created. Knowledge is dynamic and context based.

Wisdom: makes use of knowledge to create value through educated and informed decision making. Wisdom uses context to support common-sense judgement.

Concept: The Service Knowledge Management System (SKMS)

The SKMS is *"a set of tools and databases that is used to manage knowledge, information and data".*

The SKMS manages information, underpinned by the CMS and CMDB(s). It includes information on areas such as user behaviour and skills, staff skills and supplier capabilities.

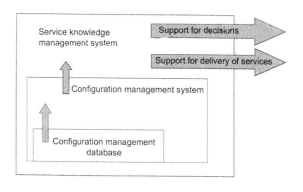

© Crown copyright 2011. Cabinet Office.

Figure 18: Relationship of the CMDB, the CMS and the SKMS

The SKMS also includes other service management information, e.g. the Service Portfolio, Service Catalogue, SLAs and OLAs.

Release and Deployment Management (RDM)

Purpose and objectives:

- Plan, schedule and control the build test and deployment of releases

- Deliver new functionality to the business whilst protecting existing services

- Ensure that the implementation of service transitions is carried out with as little disruption as possible.

Release: *"one or more changes to an IT service that are built, tested and deployed together"*.

Releases may include changes to hardware, software, documentation, processes and other components. RDM will create and agree release and deployment plans with customers and stakeholders, and create and test release packages made up of CIs.

A release package is *"a set of configuration items that will be built, tested and deployed together as a single release"*.

Release packages are stored in the DML and deployed as scheduled. RDM keeps stakeholders informed of progress and records any issues. The process will also carry out knowledge transfer for customers and support staff, and manage early life support.

Scope

Any actions needed to package, build, test and deploy a release, including systems, processes and functions.

The scope must include formal handover to Service Operation.

RDM will not:

- Physically carry out testing – this must be done independently
- Authorise changes
- Undertake work without Change Management authorisation.

Concept: Release Policy

Release Policies are defined for one or more services, and provide guidance on how to carry out a release. They include:

- Naming and numbering conventions
- Roles and responsibilities
- Release frequency
- Criteria for Service Operation handover.

The Release Policy also outlines three types of release:

- **Major releases:** affect large parts of the infrastructure. For example, a new operating system.
- **Minor releases:** affect smaller areas. For example, a software update issued to one office.
- **Emergency releases:** typically triggered by an emergency change. For example, an anti-virus update.

RDM activities

RDM has four phases:

- **Release and Deployment planning:** requires Change Management authorisation to start. Planning completes when Change Management authorises the release to be created based on the plans.

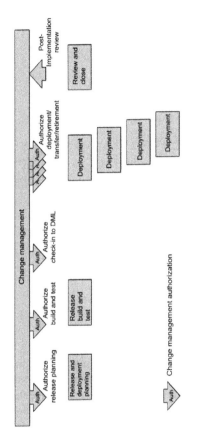

© Crown copyright 2011. Cabinet Office.

Figure 19: Phases of release and deployment management

- **Release build and test:** the release package is built, tested and placed in the DML. This phase completes when SACM is authorised to add the package to the DML, and should only happen once per release.

- **Deployment:** the package is moved from the DML to the live environment, authorised by Change Management. A release might have more than one deployment, and this phase ends when Service Operation accept the release.

- **Review and close:** lessons learnt and feedback are added to the SKMS. Performance targets are assessed to make sure they were met.

Transition Planning and Support

Purpose and objectives

This process co-ordinates transition planning and resources.

Objectives include:

- Plan and co-ordinate resources, and co-ordinate activities across teams

- Make sure that cost, quality or time estimates are met

- Create a framework of reusable practices and documents

- Make sure that plans are produced and available to customers and stakeholders as required

- Provide risk management across processes and transitions.

- Monitor and improve the performance of Service Transition processes.

Scope

This includes guiding changes through the Service Transition processes and co-ordinating resources and workloads. Priorities need to be managed across changes.

The process works with programme and project management teams, Service Design and development teams to make sure that value designed into services is transitioned into operations.

It will plan the budget and resources required and try to improve Service Transition performance.

CHAPTER 10: SERVICE OPERATION

Concept: The importance of communication

Service Operation is often made up of a number of different functions and roles, covering long service hours, including out-of-hours support.

Service Operation ensures that communication between functional areas and different shifts is managed. Good communication between functions and roles will help Service Operation to maintain service levels and meet business requirements. Service Operation communication includes:

- Handover reports
- Logs
- Timesheets
- Work flows
- Incident updates
- Other reports.

Service Operation has a lot of contact with users. All communication needs to be checked to make sure it's appropriate for the audience and useful.

Good communication can actually prevent or mitigate issues. Organisations should develop an overall communication policy to provide guidance.

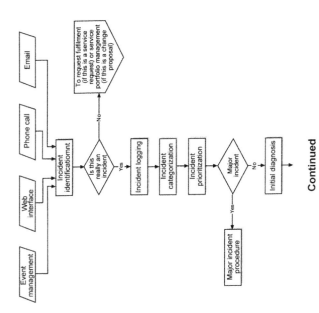

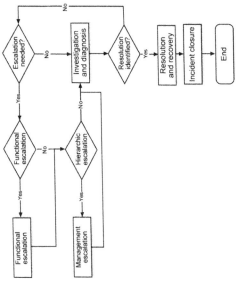

© Crown copyright 2011. Cabinet Office.

Figure 20: Incident management process flow

Service Operation processes

Incident Management

Purpose and objectives

To restore normal service as quickly as possible – minimising the down time and impact on the business. Normal service is defined in SLAs and service targets.

Objectives include:

- Using standard methods and procedures to optimise incident handling
- Improving incident communication for IT and business staff
- Improving IT's reputation by professional incident management
- Prioritising incidents according to business needs
- Maintaining user satisfaction with service quality

Scope

Incidents are reported by users, technical staff, third parties, monitoring tools and other processes, e.g. Event Management.

The Incident Management process

Process Step	Explanation
Triggers	Triggers can be received by web, monitoring tool, phone call, e-mail or user visit.
Incident Identification	Once the incident has been identified, the Service Desk will raise an incident record.
Is it an incident?	Service requests aren't handled in the same way as incidents. They will be handled by the Request Fulfilment process, and have different SLA targets.
Incident Logging	Every incident is recorded to support trend analysis and reporting. Organisations might allow users to log their own incidents via a web front-end.
Incident Categorisation	Categorisation groups incidents; for example, as hardware or software. The correct categorisation is important for assigning the incident to the correct support team and also for

	producing accurate reports.
Incident Prioritisation	Priority is based on impact and urgency.
	Impact is calculated by looking at information like the users affected, or the service criticality.
	Urgency is a measure of how quickly the business needs the resolution.
	Impact x Urgency = Priority. Prioritisation shows support teams what to fix first.
Major Incident?	Major incidents have severe impact and urgency and involve additional management resources during resolution.
Initial Diagnosis	The Service Desk will attempt a first time fix, often while the user is on the phone.
Functional/ Hierarchical Escalation	Functional and Hierarchical Escalation can be invoked at any point.
	Functional Escalation refers to incident progress from Function to Function (e.g. 2nd line support to 3rd line support).
	Hierarchical Escalation is escalation up the

	management chain, possibly to get more resources or visibility.
Investigation and Diagnosis	Carried out by appropriate resolver group.
Resolution and Recovery	This is the restoration of service to the user. The incident status is typically set to resolved, and returns to the Service Desk for closure.
Incident Closure	The only functional area that closes incidents is the Service Desk, with permission from the user. This final contact makes the incident lifecycle a closed loop process and ensures users are satisfied. Resolver teams will assign the incident to the Service Desk after resolution. Incidents need to be tracked throughout their lifecycle.

Table 4: Incident Management process

Concept: Incident

"An unplanned interruption to an IT Service – or a reduction in the quality of an IT Service. The failure of a CI that has not yet had any effect on a service is also an incident."

Concept: Incident model

Models allow similar incidents to be managed efficiently. Incident models include predefined steps, roles, responsibilities, timescales and escalation procedures.

Some incidents require precautions (like a back-up) or evidence preservation – this will also be documented in the model.

Incidents must be managed according to business criticality, with timescales for each stage of the incident lifecycle defined and agreed in OLAs and contracts to support the overall SLA.

Interfaces

Service Design processes:

- SLM: SLAs will help incident prioritisation, and Incident Management can provide an early warning of potential SLA breaches
- Capacity or Availability Management: Incidents may be related to a lack of capacity or indicate loss of availability and so supporting information is provided
- Information Security Management: security related incidents need to be managed and fed back to Service Design for future improvement.

Service Transition processes:

- SACM: the CMS is used to aid incident investigation and resolution. Incident Management can help Configuration Management identify poorly performing CIs

- Change Management: changes may be needed to resolve incidents, and incidents may be linked to failed changes.

Service Operation processes:

- Problem Management: this process uses incident records for trend analysis
- Access Management: incidents may be related to unauthorised access or security breaches. Incident history can be used to support security investigations.

Event Management

Purpose and objectives

Event Management manages events through their lifecycle including detection, analysis and response.

Event: *"any change of state that has significance for the management of a CI or service".*

Events are managed by alerts, which are ways of notifying people who need to take action. An alert is *"a notification that a threshold has been reached, something has changed or a failure has occurred".*

Events can trigger many operational processes and activities, and need to be managed and prioritised in a similar way to incidents.

Event Management forms the basis of operational monitoring and control. The process will:

- Detect changes of state
- Determine the appropriate control action

- Provide the trigger for many service management processes
- Provide information to compare service performance against SLAs
- Provide a basis for service reporting and improvement.

Scope

Event Management applies to any aspect of service management that needs to be controlled and can be automated, including:

- CIs
- Environmental systems
- Software licence monitoring
- Security
- Normal activity.

Concept: Event Categorisation

Events are divided into three categories:

- **Informational:** require no action, stored for future reference. For example, back-up job complete at 18.00 hours.
- **Warning:** signify unusual but not exceptional operation, assessed to see if action is required. For example, back-up job took 30 minutes longer than usual.
- **Exception:** a threshold has been breached or exceeded, usually meaning a service is not working as it should, or an SLA or OLA may have been breached. Action will be required,

including possible escalation to Incident, Problem or Change Management. For example, back-up job failed.

Request Fulfilment

Purpose and objectives

Service request: a *"formal request from a user for something to be provided"* – they are not incidents or failures. They are often small/standard changes, such as a request for access to an application, or a request for a laptop.

The process will manage the lifecycle of service requests – from initial enquiry through to completion and fulfilment. Request Fulfilment also manages third-party suppliers or procurement resources involved in fulfilling the request.

Objectives:

- Maintain customer and user satisfaction through efficient and professional handling of service requests
- Provide a channel for users to request and receive standard services
- Provide information to users and customers on services available and how to order them
- Source and deliver services
- Assist with general information, complaints and comments.

Scope

Service requests are usually received by Service Desk staff. Many teams can be involved in fulfilling a service request. The process tracks and manages these activities.

Incidents and service requests both need to follow the appropriate process. Request Fulfilment makes sure the Incident and Change Management processes don't get overloaded.

Access Management

Purpose and objectives

The process provides rights for users to access services, using policies set by Information Security Management during Service Design.

Objectives:

- Manage access to services based on security policies
- Respond to access requests
- Change or restrict access when needed
- Monitor access for abuse.

Scope

Access Management protects organisational data and intellectual property, including confidentiality, integrity and availability.

Problem Management

Purpose and objectives

Problem Management manages problems through their lifecycle to minimise business impact. It will also proactively try to reduce incident volumes.

The process tries to identify and remove the root cause of incidents.

Objectives include:

- Preventing problems and the resulting incidents
- Eliminating recurring incidents
- Minimising the impact of incidents.

Scope

This includes:

- Diagnosing incident root cause
- Resolving problems
- Following procedures to implement resolutions
- Maintaining process records and information
- Carrying out reactive and proactive activities
- Conducting major incident reviews
- Using techniques and analysis to support problem investigation
- Working with CSI and other processes as required.

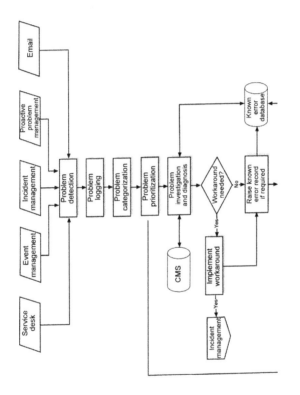

Continued

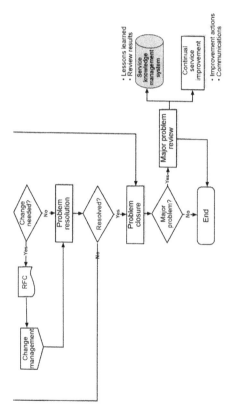

© Crown copyright 2011. Cabinet Office.

Figure 21: Problem management process flow

Concept: Problem

The unknown/underlying or root cause of one or more incidents.

Concept: Workaround

A temporary fix, made available to Incident Management to support incident resolution. May also be shared with users via a Knowledge Base.

Concept: Known Error (KE)

"A problem that has a documented root cause and a workaround."

Typically raised when the workaround and root cause have been identified, but may be reported by development teams or suppliers. KE records are stored in the Known Error Database.

Known Error Database (KEDB)

Source of workarounds for the Service Desk, also used by SACM.

Problem Management will create an RFC to remove the KE and prevent further incidents. An RFC may also be required for the workaround.

Problem Management may create problem models to deal with particular types of problem.

Problem Management activities

Problem Management has reactive and proactive activities.

- **Reactive Problem Management:** works to identify the root causes of incidents and remove them

- **Proactive Problem Management:** tries to prevent incidents before they happen – leading to an improved service for the business. Proactive techniques work to identify weak spots within the infrastructure, or perhaps try to stop problems in one area happening again elsewhere. It has strong links to CSI.

Step	Explanation
Problem Detected	Sources include: Service Desk, suppliers, trend analysis of incident records.
Problem Logged	Details include: who is affected, when and where it happened. The record will be date and time stamped.
Categorization	Likely to be the same as incident categories, for cross-referencing.
Prioritisation	Based on Impact and Urgency. The number of incidents related to a problem affects the impact.
Investigation and Diagnosis	Carried out by technical teams, with supervision from Problem Management. Analytical techniques are used to try and determine

	the root cause.
Workaround?	If a workaround is established it will be documented and shared with Incident Management.
Create Known Error Record	Once a workaround is in place, a Known Error Record is opened for informational purposes. A Known Error is typically not opened until a workaround is in place and the root cause has been established, but it can in theory be opened at any time.
Change Needed?	RFC raised if necessary.
Resolution	The resolution is implemented, and monitored to make sure the problem has been eliminated.
Closure	The problem is closed with relevant updates.
Major Problem Review	Held if needed to document any lessons learnt or actions.

Table 5: Problem Management activities

Value

Problem Management increases IT service quality. Eliminating problems reduces incidents, making users and IT staff more productive. The cost of support may also be reduced.

Interfaces

Interfaces include:

- Financial Management: helps to calculate the cost impact and pain value

- Availability and Capacity Management: support Problem Management when investigating issues related to availability or capacity; share measurements and information

- ITSCM: may be triggered by an unresolved problem

- Service Level Management: provides targets and information to support prioritisation; uses information from Problem Management in service reports and reviews

- Change Management: assesses/approves RFCs for permanent fixes and workarounds

- SACM: the CMS is used for problem investigation

- Release and Deployment Management: deploys problem fixes

- Knowledge Management: the SKMS can store the KEDB and hold or link to problem records

- Incident Management: provides incident records

- Seven-Step Improvement Process: works with Problem Management to identify improvement opportunities.

Service Operation functions

Four SO functions help to structure support resources, so that SO processes are managed correctly.

The Service Desk

Objectives:

- Restore normal service to users as quickly as possible
- Provide a single point of contact
- Use Incident Management and Request Fulfilment.

The Service Desk owns incidents throughout their lifecycle, provides excellent customer service and a level of first-time fix aligned with business requirements.

A good Service Desk leads to:

- Better customer satisfaction and perception
- Improved teamwork, communication and service focus
- Better use of support resources
- Faster turnaround of incidents and requests
- Better management information about services.

Service Desk responsibilities

Responsibilities include:

- Logging incidents and requests

- Providing first-line support
- Closing incidents with confirmation from users
- Communicating with users, including satisfaction surveys
- Updating the CMS under SACM control.

A good Service Desk will improve the reputation of the whole IT department.

Service Desk structures

Local:

- Located near the users they serve
- Help to build good relationships with users
- May be less cost efficient than centralised
- A risk that individual local working practices can develop leading to a loss of consistency
- May be justified due to different languages, cultures and time zones, etc.
- Specialised services or VIP users may need a local desk.

Centralised:

- In a single or a small number of locations
- Supports the whole organisation
- Can be very resource efficient and cost effective
- Some form of local presence may still be required for hardware fixes, etc.
- Staff can develop better skills and knowledge of frequently occurring incidents.

Virtual:

- Use technology and tools to give the impression of a single Service Desk

- Resources can be located anywhere

- Staff can work from home, be offshore or onshore

- From the user perspective they still call a single phone number and receive a consistent level of service.

Follow the sun:

- Organisations can combine Service Desks to create a 'follow the sun' desk

- The organisation takes advantage of geographical and global locations to create a 24-hour service

- Changing time zones provide 24-hour coverage more cheaply

- Analysts all need to have access to the same tool, processes and working practices.

Specialised Service Desk groups:

Groups can be created containing staff with specialised skills. Calls can be routed to different staff allowing incidents to be resolved faster. These groups are usually only implemented for key services, and where financially justified.

Technical Management

Role

Includes groups, departments and teams that provide technical expertise and manage IT infrastructure. The role includes two areas:

- Custodian of technical knowledge for managing infrastructure – including design, test, management and improvement
- Provision of resources to support the service lifecycle – making sure that resources are trained and deployed to the right areas.

Technical Management needs to balance the skill level, usage and cost of resources. Specialised resources are expensive, so their time needs to be used productively.

Objectives include:

- To plan, implement and maintain a stable infrastructure to support the business
- To create a well-designed, resilient and cost-effective environment
- To use technical skills to maintain the infrastructure, and resolve any incidents that occur.

Application Management

Role

Helps to design, deploy, manage and support applications, whether internally developed or externally procured. They manage knowledge and provide support resources.

The function has a link to Service Design to ensure new applications are fit for purpose and use. It is the custodian of technical knowledge related to applications, and helps to decide whether to 'buy or build'. It provides resources throughout the service lifecycle.

Application management balances the skills, cost and usage of resources. It guides IT Operations in managing applications on a daily basis, and makes sure application management is integrated into the full service lifecycle.

Objectives

The function ensures applications support business objectives – are well designed, resilient and cost effective with the correct functionality. They maintain applications and resolve failures.

Application development and management

Application development is a set of activities focused on creating an application solution. It is normally undertaken as a project, and the staff involved might not have much understanding of the operational environment the application will be deployed into. Application management is ongoing, and oversees and manages applications through their whole lifecycle. It uses ongoing processes, and the staff involved might find it hard to get involved with development projects as their role is seen as operational.

The goals of the two areas can be very different – application development is focused on getting a solution in place on time (the software development lifecycle), whereas application management is focused on delivering a stable application to the customer through ongoing operation and improvement. This can be seen as development having a utility focus, and management having a utility and warranty focus.

Recent trends have been to combine application development and management – combining operational and design roles. For this to work, the business needs a single point of communication, staff need updated roles and targets, and a single Change Management process needs to span both areas.

IT Operations Management

Uses processes and activities to maintain the infrastructure while identifying improvements and resolving faults. Divides into IT Operations Control and Facilities Management.

Objectives:

- Improve service and reduce cost without affecting stability
- Use skills to respond to failures.

Role

IT Operations Control carries out routine tasks including:

- Console management and operations bridge management
- Job scheduling and management
- Back-up and restore
- Print management for large jobs

- Maintenance.

Facilities Management includes:

- Management of physical IT environments
- Large-scale operational projects, e.g. server consolidation.

To be effective, IT Operations must understand:

- How technology links to services, and how performance affects services
- Procedures and guidance on technology management
- What targets have been achieved
- How cost can be optimised and reduced
- How value is more important than cost.

CHAPTER 11: CONTINUAL SERVICE IMPROVEMENT (CSI)

The CSI approach

CSI needs to be co-ordinated and managed, so tasks are not duplicated or missed.

The CSI approach includes questions that can be asked from a business and IT perspective to identify what to improve and how.

- What is the vision? Identifies long-term goals.
- Where are we now? Gives a snapshot of the organisation.
- Where do we want to be? Provides measurable, prioritised targets.
- How do we get there? Plans improvements.
- Did we get there? Uses measures to track progress.
- How do we keep momentum going? Maintains the focus on improvement.

Measurement

Measurement shows where to improve and if improvements have worked.

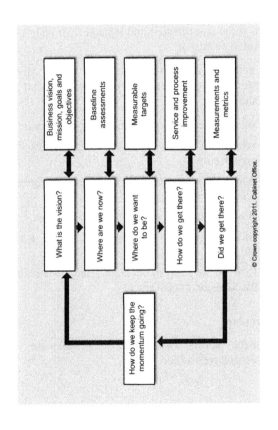

Figure 22: Continual service improvement approach

© Crown copyright 2011. Cabinet Office.

CSI focuses on three types of metrics:

- **Process:** shows if a process is meeting targets/adding value. For example, % of successful changes.

- **Service:** measures end-to-end performance. For example, availability of a service.

- **Technology:** measures infrastructure components. For example, reliability of a server.

Baselines

Progress is measured against baselines – they are a marker or start point for future comparison.

Baselines need to be accepted by all stakeholders, and should be defined at the strategic, tactical and operational levels.

If no data or previous baselines exist, the first measurements taken are the first baseline.

Metrics, Critical Success Factors and Key Performance Indicators

Metric: *"something that needs to be measured and reported to help manage a process, IT service or activity".*

Key Performance Indicator (KPI): *"A metric that is used to help manage an IT service, process, plan, project or other activity. Key performance indicators are used to measure the achievement of critical success factors. Many metrics may be measured, but only the most important of these are defined as key performance indicators and used to actively manage and report on the* *process, IT service or activity. They should be selected to ensure that efficiency, effectiveness and cost effectiveness are all managed."*

Critical Success Factor (CSF): *"Something that must happen if an IT service, process, plan, project or other activity is to succeed. Key performance indicators are used to measure the achievement of each critical success factor."*

KPIs must be related to CSFs. CSFs will be defined as high-level goals and then measured and tracked. Each CSF normally has two to three KPIs.

Here's an example CSF, KPI and metric relationship:

- CSF: Improve service performance

- KPI: Reduction in number of outage incidents

- Metrics: previous and current incident records.

Qualitative KPIs relate to service quality, e.g. an increase in customer satisfaction

Quantitative KPIs measure tangible factors, e.g. the cost of service provision

Service providers need a mix of both types of KPIs. All KPIs should be reviewed regularly to ensure they are fit for purpose, measured correctly and relevant.

The Deming Cycle

This model can be used to support CSI. It is a way of achieving higher quality and productivity popularised by W. Edwards Deming. Its four main activities are Plan, Do, Check and Act.

The Deming Cycle is critical at two points during CSI:

- Implementation of improvements
- Application of improvements to service management processes

Deming allows improvements to be planned, implemented, reviewed and refined. Maturity levels and timescales are an important part of the cycle. It is based on incremental improvements, not huge changes that the organisation may struggle to cope with.

The Cycle has a process-led approach, with consolidation steps to ensure progress is not lost.

- **Plan:** identify objectives and processes to deliver results and meet business needs
- **Do:** implement processes
- **Check:** monitor and measure
- **Act:** continually improve performance.

The Seven-Step Improvement Process

Used to identify and collect information to support improvement, the process interacts with the Deming Cycle and DIKW progression.

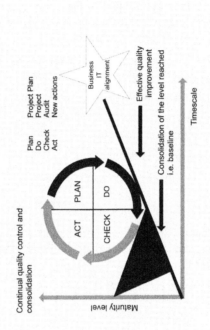

Figure 23: Plan-do-check-act cycle

© Crown copyright 2011. Cabinet Office.

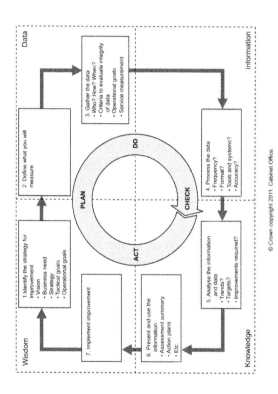

© Crown copyright 2011. Cabinet Office.

Figure 24: The seven-step improvement process

Purpose and objectives

The process defines and manages the steps that identify, define, gather, process, present and implement improvements.

Every potential improvement opportunity will need a business case justification to show the overall business benefit.

Objectives include:

- Identify improvements
- Reduce the cost of service provision
- Align services with business requirements
- Identify measures to justify improvement
- Review services and service achievement
- Understand what to measure and why.

Scope

The scope includes analysis of the performance and capabilities of services, processes, partners and technology across the lifecycle. Technology use is optimised and services can be aligned with business needs.

The organisational structure, roles and staff capabilities and skills are also in scope.

Activities

Step 1: Identify the strategy for improvement, including vision, business need, strategic, tactical and operational goals.

Step 2: Define what you will measure. Service Strategy and Design identify this earlier in the lifecycle. CSI identifies the real situation and conducts a gap analysis.

Step 3: Gather the data – normally from Service Operation monitoring of live services.

Step 4: Process the data, in line with CSFs and KPIs. Raw data needs to be rationalised and standardised.

Step 5: Analyse information and data, including asking who, what, when, where, how questions. Trends provide a credible message to present to management, but this step is often rushed or overlooked.

Step 6: Present and use the information. Careful presentation supports decision making, with appropriate information presented to different stakeholder groups.

Step 7: Implement improvements to correct, optimise or improve services and processes. Wisdom is applied to knowledge to get the right solution.

After Step 7, a new baseline is taken and the process recommences.

The CSI register

The CSI register records improvement opportunities – some will be implemented now, others later and some may never be delivered. The register ensures they are recorded and tracked.

- Improvement opportunities are categorised into small, medium and large tasks
- They are grouped into quick wins, medium-term undertakings and long-term solutions
- Improvement can be prioritised and resources allocated appropriately

- Register forms part of the SKMS, giving structure and visibility
- Can be linked to organisational KPIs
- Owned by the CSI manager.

CHAPTER 12: ROLES

There are a number of generic roles that support a service management organisational structure.

Process owner

Accountable for ensuring a process is fit for purpose and performing adequately. A process owner has to be a single person or role, to avoid duplication or confusion.

Accountabilities include:

- Defining process strategy, policies and standards
- Assisting with process design, including metrics
- Providing resources and ensuring they understand their role
- Making sure the process is documented
- Auditing the process
- Addressing issues or opportunities for improvement.

Process manager

Accountable for operational management of a process. There may be more than one manager per process (for example, one change manager in each office), or the manager and owner roles may be combined in smaller organisations.

Accountabilities include:

- Working with the process owner
- Ensuring process activities are carried out

- Appointing staff to roles and managing resources
- Monitoring and reporting on process performance
- Working with service owners and other process managers to make sure processes support services
- Identifying improvements and working with the CSI manager to prioritise them
- Making improvements to process implementation.

Process practitioner

The role may be combined with the process manager, or there may be multiple practitioners per process.

Responsibilities include:

- Carrying out process activities
- Understanding how their role links to services and creates value
- Working with other stakeholders
- Making sure that inputs, outputs and interfaces are correct
- Creating or updating records of their activities.

Service owner

Accountable for delivery of an IT service. They may not carry out all activities, but they will make sure work is completed.

Responsibilities include:

- Responsible to the customer for service initiation, transition, maintenance and support
- Accountable to the IT director for service delivery
- Attending CAB and internal and external service review meetings
- Communicating with customers about the service
- Serving as a point of escalation
- Participating in SLA and OLA negotiations
- Interfacing with service management processes, particularly BRM.

The RACI Model

Used to manage roles and resources during a piece of work or task. Provides a clear mapping of roles across different teams in the organisation.

RACI includes:

- Responsible: one or more resources who carry out tasks, reporting to the accountable resource
- Accountable: only one person, with overall authority for the task
- Consulted: resources (people, documents, etc.) that have information required for the task
- Informed: resources who need an output from the task or need to know how it is progressing.

When applied to processes, the process owner will be accountable for every activity within the process – even if they are not carrying them out.

CHAPTER 13: SERVICE MANAGEMENT AUTOMATION

Automation can improve service asset performance, and service utility and warranty:

- Automated resources can have their capacity adjusted easily
- They don't need human intervention, so can be available across time zones or service hours
- Automated systems can be measured and improved
- Computers can optimise services and processes in ways that humans could not
- Automation can capture knowledge about a process, and share it more easily.

Service process automation delivers benefits including:

- Better service quality
- Reduced costs and risks
- Reduced complexity and uncertainty.

These service management areas benefit from automation:

- Design and modelling
- Service Catalogue
- Pattern recognition and analysis
- Classification, prioritisation and routing
- Detection and monitoring
- Optimisation.

Planning for automation

Consider these four steps when planning for automation:

- Simplify processes
- Clarify processes
- Make automated systems simple for the end-user
- Accept some processes can't be automated.

CHAPTER 14: SERVICE MANAGEMENT SKILLS AND TRAINING

Service management staff need the right skills. They need to understand business priorities and how IT supports them, possess customer service skills and have the ability to innovate.

Generic service management role requirements could include:

- Management skills
- Meeting management skills
- Communication skills – written and verbal
- Negotiation skills
- Analytical mind-set.

Standard roles and job titles help to manage roles and responsibilities. Organisations can adopt frameworks like the Skills Framework for the Information Age (*www.sfia.org.uk*).

CHAPTER 15: THE ITIL QUALIFICATION SCHEME

The scheme has four levels:

- Foundation – mandatory, two credits
- Intermediate – based on Lifecycle and Capability streams, then the mandatory Managing Across the Lifecycle
- Expert – granted once candidates achieves 22 credits
- Master.

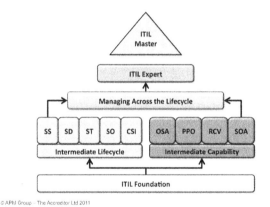

Figure 25: The ITIL qualification scheme

Read more at *www.itil-officialsite.com*.

CHAPTER 16: THE FOUNDATION EXAM

- 40 multiple-choice questions
- 60 minutes
- 65% or 26/40 to pass
- No trick questions
- Closed book.

You can download the Foundation Syllabus and a free sample exam from the ITIL Official Site: *www.itil-officialsite.com*.

A full ITIL glossary of terms is also available in multiple languages from the site.

ITG RESOURCES

IT Governance Ltd. sources, creates and delivers products and services to meet the real-world, evolving IT governance needs of today's organisations, directors, managers and practitioners.

The ITG website (*www.itgovernance.co.uk*) is the international one-stop-shop for corporate and IT governance information, advice, guidance, books, tools, training and consultancy.

http://www.itgovernance.co.uk/itil.aspx is the information page on our website for ITIL resources.

Other Websites

Books and tools published by IT Governance Publishing (ITGP) are available from all business booksellers and are also immediately available from the following websites:

http://www.itgovernance.eu is our euro-denominated website which ships from Benelux and has a growing range of books in European languages other than English.

www.itgovernanceusa.com is a US dollar-based website that delivers the full range of IT Governance products to North America, and ships from within the continental US.

www.itgovernanceasia.com provides a selected range of ITGP products specifically for customers in the Indian sub-continent.

www.itgovernance.asia delivers the full range of ITGP publications, serving countries across Asia Pacific. Shipping from Hong Kong, US dollars, Singapore dollars, Hong Kong dollars, New Zealand dollars and Thai baht are all accepted through the website.

www.27001.com is the IT Governance Ltd. website that deals specifically with information security management, and ships from within the continental US.

Toolkits

ITG's unique range of toolkits includes the IT Governance Framework Toolkit, which contains all the tools and guidance that you will need in order to develop and implement an appropriate IT governance framework for your organisation. Full details can be found at *www.itgovernance.co.uk/products/519*.

For a free paper on how to use the proprietary Calder-Moir IT Governance Framework, and for a free trial version of the toolkit, see
www.itgovernance.co.uk/calder_moir.aspx.

There is also a wide range of toolkits to simplify implementation of management systems, such as an ISO/IEC 27001 ISMS or an ISO/IEC 22301 BCMS, and these can all be viewed and purchased online at: *http://www.itgovernance.co.uk/catalog/1*.

Training Services

IT Governance offers an extensive portfolio of training courses designed to educate information security, IT governance, risk management and compliance professionals. Our classroom and online training programmes will help you develop the skills required to deliver best practice and compliance to your organisation. They will also enhance your career by providing you with industry-standard certifications and increased peer recognition. Our range of courses offers a structured learning path from foundation to advanced level in the key topics of information security, IT governance, business continuity and service management.

ISO/IEC 20000 is the first international standard for IT service management and has been developed to reflect the best practice guidance contained within the ITIL framework. Our ISO20000 Foundation and Practitioner training courses are designed to provide delegates with a comprehensive introduction and guide to the implementation of an ISO20000 management system and an industry-recognised qualification awarded by APMG International.

Full details of all IT Governance training courses can be found at *http://www.itgovernance.co.uk/training.aspx*.

Professional Services and Consultancy

As IT service management becomes ever more important in organisations, so the deployment of best practice (e.g. ITIL), or the development of a management system that can be certified to ISO/IEC 20000, becomes a greater challenge; especially when the management systems have to be integrated to achieve the most cost-effective and efficient corporate structure.

IT Governance has substantial real-world experience as a professional services company specialising in IT GRC-related management systems. Our consulting team can help you to design and deploy IT service management structures, such as ITIL and ISO20000, and integrate them with other systems, such as ISO/IEC 27001, ISO22301, ISO14001 and COBIT®. Like ITIL itself, we pride ourselves in being vendor neutral and nonprescriptive in our mentoring approach, transferring the knowledge that you need to document, challenge and improve.

For more information about IT Governance consultancy for IT service management, see: *http://www.itgovernance.co.uk/itsm-itil-iso20000-consultancy.aspx*.

Publishing Services

IT Governance Publishing (ITGP) is the world's leading IT-GRC publishing imprint that is wholly owned by IT Governance Ltd.

With books and tools covering all IT governance, risk and compliance frameworks, we are the publisher of choice for authors and distributors alike, producing unique and practical publications of the highest quality, in the latest formats available, which readers will find invaluable.

www.itgovernancepublishing.co.uk is the website dedicated to ITGP, enabling both current and future authors, distributors, readers and other interested parties to have easier access to more information, allowing them to keep up to date with the latest publications and news from ITGP.

Newsletter

IT governance is one of the hottest topics in business today, not least because it is also the fastest moving.

 You can stay up to date with the latest developments across the whole spectrum of IT governance subject matter, including risk management, information security, ITIL and IT service management, project governance, compliance and so much more, by subscribing to ITG's core publications and topic alert e-mails. Simply visit our subscription centre and select your preferences:
www.itgovernance.co.uk/newsletter.aspx.

CPSIA information can be obtained
at www.ICGtesting.com
Printed in the USA
BVOW06s1147050117
472581BV00008B/30/P